Demons to Face

My book of poems is filled with love and despair. Each page will bring something different to the plate. I started this book when I was sixteen and finished it when I was eighteen; During this timeline I have changed - so the way emotions, tones, and words are expressed will vary throughout Demons to Face.

By the everlasting student Ishmael

Publisher: Ishmael K. Staples

Copyright Year: ©2018 Ishmael Kain Staples

ISBN-13: 978-0-578-57983-2

Table of contents

1. Love Notes
2. High School Idiots
3. No One Can Hear You
4. Demons to Face
5. Her Laugh
6. The Stars in Her Eyes
7. The Outcast
8. Her Lips
9. Running Through Time
10. Into The Hearts of Humans
11. Dreams to Distractions
12. Meaningless Things
13. A Castle to Hide In
14. The Descent into Sadness
15. Her Eyes Shine
16. The Only One I Need
17. This Is Me
18. The Look in Your Eyes
19. Demons at my Throat
20. Lions Bellies Roar
21. One You Love Forever
22. Sitting Three Fourths Full
23. This Moment Won't Last Forever
24. Caught Up and Tied Up
25. Friends Who Used to Be
26. You're All I Think About
27. You See Me
28. Death Shall be our Beginning
29. A Kiss is What Started This
30. Silence in Sitting
31. The Teeth of a Captor
32. Life Fades in Horror
33. Rest for the Wicked
34. A World of Demons
35. Alone to be Forgotten
36. Theories of a Deadman
37. Love is my Reward
38. The Side Effects of Being Human
39. Out of Misery
40. Being Tugged Around
41. The Angel That Takes us Down
42. We are Human
43. For Mothers and Their Sons
44. Greed is in Our Nature
45. As our Maker Sees Things
46. The Last Hope
47. All We Inherit May be Pain
48. Frozen Over
49. On a different spectrum of light
50. Self-Medication
51. My Bleeding Eyes
52. Insane to a point
53. Recipe for Disaster
54. What is so good about being Human
55. The simple mind of a world
56. Final Goodbye

with some surprises here and there.

Love Notes

Sitting waiting

Looking and wondering who wrote you this ominous note

Asking you to meet them here

You go through list of people you would like it to be

Then you go through list of who you wouldn't want it to be

Then inconspicuously you see out the corner of your eye the shy

person who's always in the back of the room

Who keeps to themselves

You wonder why they are here

Then you realize they are waiting for a ride

So you go to the worst option the one who left the note isn't coming

As you wait ten, twelve, twenty minutes

No one comes you walk away feeling like a fool

Yet they are sitting there watching you to scared to come out from

behind that corner

High School Idiots

There they are

All you want to do is slam their face into the concrete

Make their teeth fall out

Make them realize that screwing with you was a bad idea

You think of all the ways you can kill them

Yet you hold back

You let your anger simmer out

No need to waste it on nobodies

Burger flippers, and stay at home druggies

So let them talk as you slowly leave and they sit in the same place they

were at in high school

No One can Hear You

You shout

Yet it's like a void took your breath away

No one can hear you

No one can see you writhing in pain

The agony of it is you help others shout and can't help yourself

So you sit there yelling into nothing

Hoping to get past the barrier that haunts you

No one notices or they are just dealing with their own

To the point they won't notice you

So scream and shout but we aren't getting out

Demons to Face

Brawling with despair

You hear others shouting but you can't hear what they are saying

They scream but they are inaudible

All you hear is the beast you are fighting

With a smile on your face

This fight you can't win as it towers over

Tears fill your eyes as the hole in the ground deepens

You feel it hit your shoe almost making you trip

You look to others for help

But they have their own demons to face

So you hold yours off with one arm and help those around you

Yet they don't notice the one you are facing so you fight your beast alone

Letting its anger seep into your skin.

Her Laugh

You can hear that laugh from a mile away

Light, soft and soothing

She coos softly in my ear

I know it isn't because I'm funny

I know it's because I am goofy and can't hit a punchline right

Yet to get that laugh I would do anything

So I smile and lean in towards her and whisper little jokes

Jokes that are cheesy and probably sound like crap

Yet every time she lets me hear that love in her laugh

Helping Others Who Hurt the Ones That Help

Am I meant to try to save everyone with a hole for everyone saved

Am I supposed to look like a man who is dead with the knives in back

Am I supposed to break helping others climb mountains

Am I the only one conscience of his actions at all times

Will i stare to oblivion at the oblivious and cradle all those I can reach or

am I just

Just a false man waiting for someone to save me instead

Looking for the deepest retinas

Looking for someone to bear joy and happiness with

Maybe i am meant to take the pain I am sent and give out love instead

Was this meant to drive my insanity

Or am I looking to hard being to stern trying to hard and not being selfish

enough

What am I?

A bridge, a hand, a shoulder, a mountain to climb on I don't know who I am

I have lost myself to try to help others and I have so far to go what

awaits me in the future I hope I won't have to feel or hear pain

anymore

I hope my future is soon

For I don't know what will happen if I have to hold out for everyone

else much longer

The Stars in Her Eyes

All I can see are the stars in her eyes

The millions of years in the past

Where all I can think about is being with her

The oceans and winds won't stop me

She has to be the one I love forever

Because no one else has those eyes

Where she is looking into and knows what you are and who you can

be

Flip the Coin

She is staring at her phone

Giving a constant glow to her face

The mystery as to why no one can talk to her

Why she is popular on her social but can't be around

Because she is checked out mentally gone vanished

Behind the drug that is her phone and the likes

Instead of looking at the person across the street

The one next to her at a shop

She can't be social and the world accepted this norm

these are your stars

The Outcast

I am alienated

Outcasted by society

Misunderstood for an idiot

Misinterpreted as an asshole

Yet those who actually get to know me know

They know I am a genius

They know I can be one of the best friends ever

They also know that if anything ever happens this alien has their

back.

Her Lips

Stuck on her lips

That's all I can remember

She probably can't even remember my name

Yet all I can think about is the way we kissed last

If it will ever happen again

And if I can keep those lips from kissing anyone else's

Because that kiss is something that draws me to her

I want her to keep kissing me like that for the rest of my life.

Running Through Time

Running through time as fast as we can

Not stopping to realize that we can't run back

To when age deceived us

Decrepit and old unable to go back

Wishing you could move like you used to

Then losing your head

Ending up in the world inside your head

You are trapped in yourself wishing for death.

Into the Hearts of Humans

Into the hearts of humans we shall descend

The dark cold unforgiving place that is man

The place where desires chase

Where lovers run

This is where they take blood from another man

Wars over this place are fought but never won

So leave the darkness for it shall come.

What About the Good Ones?

Here and there by few and far

Humans who show their hearts and actually listen to others

They look into yours eyes and understand the pain the joy the love

They exist in stories and in life

Though they disappear ever so slightly because the world

Takes advantage of this kindness and not many can keep a hold

Be careful for when they are gone so in humanity

Dreams to Distraction

Pirates, Zombies, and what all the kids like

Wonder and amusement is what we all have at 5 or 6

Yet later when the Easter Bunny, Santa and the Tooth Fairy are all

gone

We look to avoid and hide from everything

We take pills, drinks, and smokes

To get away and hope for that feeling we once felt when we were

young

MY HOPES

Glimpses of these fleeting images

Images of what could have been what could be and what may come

Fear of mistakes

Fear of things that will never happen

I wish I had singular options but there is an array with a magnitude which I can't comprehend

I wish to dive and let myself flow endlessly

But visions and dreams of wants, desires, and world consequences

Wake me from the numb pain I am dealt

Trying to create something that time cannot break, which helps those who have hurt me

I am human but have never felt to be a part of what humanity has decided humans should be

I hope my children be smart but naive to what I see and can be happy without seeing the world as I do

Without having the demons look them in the face and claim to be friends

I want more and less I don't need them to compare to me or try to do better all I want is happiness no matter if that mean blind joy or comprehending beyond what I can imagine I want their emotions to be theirs and not of the consequence from what happened in their lives

Meaningless Things

Looking around

In a group where I am the only one there

They are all looking at and saying all these meaningless things

Raised by people who only care about those things

Yet here i am looking at the universe hoping that when we die it isn't

all just gone.

A Castle to Hide In

Pushing through the walls

Running past the arrows they send at you

She has hid and built a castle to hide in

She wouldn't let you in

So you forced yourself through

Through hundreds of guards and millions of demons

This is where she runs

She runs here when she can't accept the change that you would bring

her.

The Dissent of Sadness

She comes to in a dissent of sadness

You are her rock and shoulder to lean on

Yet she won't let you hold her forever

She goes to others and won't stay with you

You beg for her to be yours

She looks at you with want

That's all she does as she runs to another to hurt her

Her Eyes Shine

Her eyes shine with intelligence

They look at you with deliberately placed desire

She wants you to come to her

She will make the oceans fill your heart

Then have the demons take your soul

She shall be the one you bless

And the one who will take you to bliss.

This is Me

Destroyed, broken, insane

This is me

No joy, happiness, love

Forgotten, outcasted

Left for the dead

Yet you expect me to owe you all some kindness or decency

Fuck you and your double standards

This is me, the truth, the fact

The one who causes rage and makes you feel inferior

So talk down to me see how that works when I am perched above you

and your petty grievances

Keep talking as I drop a branch on you from above.

The Look in Your Eyes

Betrayed by the look in your eyes

You said you were mine forever

Then you went and screwed a waste of space

Someone who isn't even worth 1 of my fingers

Yet you expect me to talk to you

To take you back after stabbing me in the back

No

Time to leave and destroy what was called a heart

I need this numbness, the pain of insanity

Now let me repeat my day to day life expecting a change

Demons at My Throat

I light up at the thought of you, yet at the edge of my vision all

I see is the darkness from me creep to hold you

Is it wrong to want you to hold me and my demons

as I see through yours which hide you look into mine seeing none

Because they are right behind you slitting my throat

Love me as you can before my demons get the cut.

Lions Bellies Roar

I hear the lion's belly rumble as

I run from myself It's slowly getting closer and the more I think

The more I want to turn and yell

This is not what I claim or want to be

Yet this world clings to it tying it, to the mask I put over it and trying

to pull my insanity through the eyes, nose, and mouth

All I can feel is run and die

Or turn and hope to survive

This decision isn't of my thinking it would be of my feeling

Yet all I can think is my way through and the way I feel breaks way to

how I think

One You Love Forever

Sorry I am not your absolute

The one you love forever

So when you want to hear my voice

Or have me by your side

All you need to do is give me a call

I will be there for you as quick as lightning

I will hold you in my arms as the sky cradles the ground

You will be what I hold dearest even if you aren't mine

Sitting Three Fourths Full

No love to me shall come

My heart shall sit three fourths full

As I watch everyone fill theirs

I sit and wait for a thing that will never come

This desire turns to rage

This rage turns to hate

This hate lasts longer than the thoughtless void

Run away before my love consumes you

This Moment Won't Last Forever

Two arrive one shall die

Consent your heart to desire

For in this moment you can't last forever

So let your last thought be broken

This one died and now you're up

Who is the one you let yourself desire

Now let the broken go and

Leave what the other did not want

Caught Up and Tied Up

I can't dream

I can't sleep

You are all I think about

You are all I want

No matter where I am I see you

There in my car smiling right before I kiss you

You keep me up and there's nothing I can do

You have me caught up, tied up

But there is nothing I want more

You

Friends Who Used to Be

Looking through two whole years of text

Wondering what went wrong why we split the group

Wondering if I was the cause of it

Or if the insanity of each other finally got us away from each other

We have all gone our separate ways

I know we hit some bumps but you can still look to me as a friend

You're All I Think About

Can't sleep

All I can do is think of you

I want you here warm next to me

Holding onto my chest in case of nightmares

Waking with frizzy hair and a tired smile

I want you there in my arms reach where I can tease and laugh at all

the little things

That I love about you

You See Me

You see my eyes

You see my body

You see my strength

You don't see my anger

You don't see the deception I weave

You don't see the danger I am

Snakes may show it in their eyes

But my danger arrives unseen and random

Death Shall be our Beginning

Come to me be the only one I need

You're the only one I want to have or love

As so I will never leave you

You will be the only one I want to hold my hand

You will be the only one for me we will make death look like marriage

and never leave

For us it won't be till death do us part It will be together forever

Through the death of earth and life we are the only ones who will be

A Kiss is What Started This

It started with a kiss

But there was nothing after

You run and hide in fear of letting me in

You built your walls

You hide from what would cause you joy

All for the sake of not letting him know you better This is you

This is how you dug your grave of despair

Silence in Sitting

Sitting in silence

Looking for a way out

Can't breathe

The collar is too tight

Is this the world for me

Did I forget what fundamentally is needed to live

Or is that I was never given the fundamentals for living

For we all shall die who is to say we lived at all

The Teeth of a Captor

Dark bitter cold and damp

You feel the teeth of your captor sinking into your throat

You feel cold syrup flow around you

The sky turns purple, red, then a golden hue

Before it all goes dark

The feeling of your captor gone

The cold syrup that flowed around you no longer there

Are you ready for the end of all known

Are you ready for the tragedy you sown yourself

Look through the thread then grasp your end

Life Fades in Horror

I look in horror as life fades

Everything looks so grey and hazed over

They sit on one legged chair in bravado

They can't understand the meaning of death

So look at how they go through life dazed and confused

Wishing they were you

Yet they can't feel an intolerable pain that is ready

Ready to burst straight through your skull

Leading you off a cliff

Rest for the Wicked

No rest for the wicked they say

Well rest comes for the forsaken and loved

Yet the wicked sleep in a world of ignorance

While the forsaken and loved give other rest without taking any

So wake with your greed, lust, and other sins

For no human is conscious of our wickedness

So we consume, see, forget repeat

As when rest comes to you think

Think of all the unseen, unconsumed, and unforgotten

For they will give you rest even in your dreams

A World of Demons

We live in a world full of demons

Not monsters you dream of or draw

No horns, no red skin, no fire for blood

They have eyes like yours

A grin and an oddly placed birthmark like yours

Hair done in the same style and clothes alike

Look into the mirror and you may see my fright

Human you may be but you're condemned

You have fears yet you're mine

Humans are the scariest living things

As living goes, we hurt and destroy more than all

So look into that mirror and see the murderer of you, I suppose

Alone to be Forgotten

Alone and forgotten

In a crowd but singled out

Made fun of and passed around

The misfit who feels little joy

The misfit with no friends

Forever alone and forgotten ask the misfit why

He shall say because of you the one I thought could understand

The one I thought could comprehend

The one who left me in a crowd

The one who deserts me for another

You're the reason a misfit destroys and carries his burdens

Unknown to all until many fall

So, help that misfit before he takes you all

Theories of a Deadman

Theory is all I have

The theory behind love

Yet you see me as a theory of a deadman

Low and misunderstood

So as I adore all of you

You set out for lights

Leaving me to my theories and explanations

Well for all these theories and explanations

I still can't come up with why I want your love

So, set me free by letting me be by you

For without you I have theories and unknowns

So be my known

P.S. I love you

Love is My Reward

My shoulder is yours

You can lean on it

Cry on it

Grab it scratch it punch it

Whatever your mood

Yet my reward for this

Is you by my shoulder forever

Through thick and thin

You shall be by me and me by you

The Side Effects of Being Human

The demons have eviscerated all you care for

Your house torn and shredded

The girl you married guts are thrown about

You go to your parents in fear

When you arrive, you find their heads on a post

Walk away hide from what is inside

Next time you look in the mirror

You will see your body torn and sown around the room

Out of Misery

Waiting for someone to come

To help put you out of your misery

To put a bullet between your teeth and an arrow in your skull

To put a rope around your neck

Well no one will what's the point

You hate yourself and look to others to do for you what you won't

Why would they come when you aren't worth their time

Listen in as hope fades

The black of despair is all you crave

Now you will be the one putting bullets in teeth

And arrows through skulls

watch out for you we shall

Being Tugged Along

Sitting in the stars

Lighting a fire

Hoping to get fingers between yours

Wishing you noticed the way I look at you

Yet you deny me time and time again

You go for others that just aren't right for you

Then you look at me and tug me along I have hope in my eyes

My heart says go with it go along with them

Yet all I can think is that I am going to get hurt again

For she has done this to me

She is doing it now

She will do it again

The Angel That Takes Us Down

Here we are falling to the angels

Their wings as dark as the pit of space

Their smiles are inviting

The way their bodies invite you as if to give bliss

The gods frown at them but you can't tell

For the light you see is in front of you while they take you down

They hold you delicately like a newborn

This is the task they have

To give you a little bliss before damning you

Before letting you sit in torture of what is to come.

We are Human

The world looks on in whoa

All it can see are the scars we have left

To her we are like parasites

We destroy the hand that feeds us

Then we take to killing what would feed us

We do it meticulously and greedily

For we have no hope to survive on a planet that harbors things like us

We kill for sport and take excess in joy

watch us as we kill each other

We are worse than parasites

We are human

For Mothers and Their Sons

I have fallen in love mother

Sorry to say it's not a girl you would ever like

She is gorgeous, cute, beautiful

She makes the sun dimmer because how bright she may be

The seas run away and the oceans turn for how independent she is

Yet you won't like her because she loves another

Even though you won't like her

All I can see are how the flowers turn and bloom for her

How angels swoon and fall to earth before her feet

So, I'm sorry my heart wasn't precautious

Just tell me that no matter how much she hurts me

You mother will be the woman I always love

Greed is in Our Nature

To the sky and treasures, I would give you

You look at me as a disgrace

Look at this world you know

For I can change its flavor with my taste

See the sky as blue but when I am done

All you shall see is grey

For you look at me as evil

But when your boy is born my inventions are what he will inspire to

beat

Beat them he shall but in doing so

You may see your son turn cold

watch the treasures and skies I may bring

For they may be like gold and cause a fever

One that makes the world tear itself apart

Just to get a sip of what I shall bring

As Our Maker Sees Things

Dull and boring as hell

You may see me as a man

But this man has made goddess's cry and god's sing

Praise I do not need

Just watch you build your cities and towns

For I will see the part where we burn

You may say that Salem was bad

But in the dreams of man

We cause our own insanity

We hurt one another so bad that Natural disasters look like patty cake

The sores and poison we spread through words, guns, and other weapons

These are what most will see as our legacy

This time our war is Fought with sticks and rocks

The Last Hope

We got addicted to the violence, the anger, the sadness

look at those just born and full of joy

For they may be the last hope to keep this dump running

Running without the help of humankind

To keep things natural and not digitized

watch them learn and fill them with joy

Because they are the last hope

The last hope the world has to keep us up

To survive without demolishing the beauty around us

All We Inherit May be Pain

We Turn and look at all the bad

Wondering why me

Asking in What we believe in

Why did you place us here

Looking at them to solve our problems

Yet if we looked at it differently

We might need these bad times

These bad times might take us somewhere

Wherever it may be good or bad

These things created us

watch yourself

Then look and wonder

Where did this side of me arrive from

Then hope it doesn't end in your version of hell

Frozen Over

My heart has Frozen over

She has left me for another

This so-called man is her lover

Hope her life is well as long as she ends up in hell

For this is where my heart shall go

To the ends of which I torture myself hoping

That she will come by and place the knife where it belongs

In my throat

On a different spectrum of light

My color has faded in your eyes

I'm a star who has no light in your spectrum

Maybe I am dark on yours

But in my spectrum, all I see may pale compared to me

watch out for what you call light may be a false sense in your eyes

For I may be as dark as space

Yet when the spectrum changes, I am purple, red, and blue

Brighter and denser than any around you

close your eyes feel what I project off

Instead of seeing what I may be in your eyes

Self-Medication

Self-medicating to get throughout the day

How is that glaze in my eye

The look of desperation on my face

Wondering who will be the next to give a ride

To make Alice's Wonderland seem like a little kids dream

Looking through a half full glass

Wondering when it will take effect

It never works out the way it is wanted to

It just sits and turns in veins

Watch the turn of rage and despair that follows

All you will see is bars after that turn

The turn through which we may all follow

My Bleeding Eyes

Look into my bleeding eyes

They show you oblivion and death

This is what the world you live in wanted

Yet when you look into my eyes

Tears run down your cheek as you complain about the unfairness of society

Just remember these eyes are because of many

These eyes have seen in the past and looked to the future

Where everything is bleak and dark

The only hope they have of clearing is if they are brought to the present

With the hope and love of a fool

Sitting on a plate for me to devour

Devour I shall for I have hope and love of a fool that humanity may thrive

Yet this thriving I want them to have has caused these pitch red eyes

Recipe for Disaster

Recipe for disaster

Humans we are

We fight

Give contempt and deceit

Smile as the monster we fear

Turn those greedy eyes away

For you may be slaughtered

By those who once were your friends and loved ones

Humans we are

But can you see the disaster you are?

What is So Good about being human

What is so great about being human

We fight, disrupt, and cause sorrow

We send others out of the herd leaving them to wallow

Not for difference but for the likeness we see in false idles

Notorious, outcasted, infamous

These describe, those we hurt

Yet when put in the dirt

You grab the dirt and throw it in another's eyes

Hoping to terrify

Now look at each other and tell me what is so good about being human

Not so much, we are demonic and angelic alike

Yet between both which has a more sinister smile

Or maybe it's the smile of some other force yet to be known

Just sit and watch the destruction we cause

Calling for the love of each other

The Simple Mind of a World

The world we have is simple minded

It drains the life out of all it creates to live a little longer

Like a drowning man that cannot swim

It sucks you in and takes all you have

We act as if we are Gods and control the state of our environment around us

Then when looking out all we see is when it decides

Decides to rock and crumble to the ground

When it does, we falter

Look at the world as if we cannot believe it

For we gave the world our all and got back

Back an ounce of our blood

Spit in our face

The world sits back laughing hard at the expression on our faces

Wonder, create, and feed

To take control and dine on

Without the world we live on

Maybe our mortality

Becomes immortality

Programmed Lives

Running

Running

Look into their dreams

None of them fight

They all cower and hide

False looks and impressions

To something inhuman they wish they were

But where is humanity without its own flavor of insanity

Rampant with people who scare themselves

Loose on themselves because of

Of unwanted effects of how they react

Just as long as they don't have to look

Into the mirror

To see their decaying look and programmed eyes

No room for anything but the possessions wanted next.

Final Goodbye

This is goodbye my one and final

For I see you no longer

For I cannot feel you no more

watch me leave and blow the dust off my shoulder

Because I am done chasing girls who can't do anything but follow

You have never decided your fate

You go for the dimwits and losers

The ones who choose drugs and others things over others

go ahead and follow, just remember

When he leaves you for another that he thinks is better

That you lost your last chance for better

So goodbye and farewell

Because I won't become your loser.

I know this is supposed to be at the beginning of the poems, but I don't really care where it is supposed to go. This goes to my family and those I love around me. If you think I'm mentally ill or something I'm sorry. Well not necessarily we are all mental a little I just found a way to describe mine a little differently. Hope you enjoyed the poems.

My thanks

Sincerely,

The Author.

www.ingramcontent.com/pod-product-compliance
Lightning Source LLC
Chambersburg PA
CBHW081354040426
42450CB00016B/3437